games people play!

India

Dale E. Howard

CHILDREN'S PRESS®
A Division of Grolier Publishing
New York • London • Hong Kong • Sydney
Danbury, Connecticut

Editorial Staff

Project Editor: Mark Friedman

Photo Research: Feldman & Associates

Design Staff

Design and Electronic Composition:
  TJS Design

Maps: TJS Design

Cover Art and Icons: Susan Kwas

Activity Page Art: MacArt Design

Library of Congress Cataloging-in-Publication Data

Howard, Dale E.
India / by Dale E. Howard.
p. cm.—(Games people play)
Includes index.
Summary: Discusses ways Indians recreate, including exercise, sports, games, folk dances, and kite flying.
ISBN 0-516-04437-0
1. Sports—India—Juvenile literature. 2. Sports—Sociological aspects—India—Juvenile literature. 3. Games—India. [1. Recreation—India. 2. Games—India. 3. Sports—India. 4. India—Social life and customs.]
I. Title. II. Series.

GV653.H68 1996   95-40248
796'.0954—dc20   CIP
                                          AC

3313/544

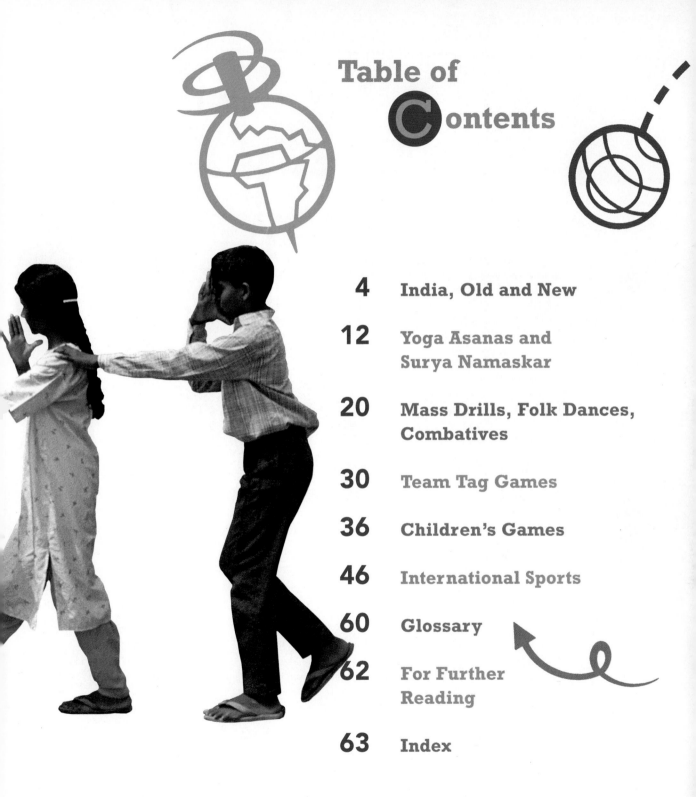

Table of **C**ontents

India, Old and New

India is full of surprises. Both a very
ancient land and a modern industrial
country, India offers sights, sounds,
and smells found nowhere else.

As you walk down a street in India, you may meet cows and buses, horse-drawn carriages called tongas and motorcycle rickshaws, wandering holy men called sadhus wearing only loincloths, businessmen sporting new suits, and women wearing richly woven silk saris. You'll see street vendors selling wares from baskets carried on their heads beside supermarkets. You'll find people reading palms, giving haircuts, or taking baths on the street. Everywhere music blares forth from radios and television sets. You'll smell incense burning in shops and shrines, sweetmeats and curries simmering in large pans on open stoves, and exhaust from cars. Everywhere you go, you will find people, people, and more people!

Holding to Hindu beliefs, many people in India treat cows with great respect.

The Taj Mahal

Ancient civilizations flourished in southern India and in the Indus River Valley about 4,500 years ago. The Indus cities of Harappa and Mohenjo-Daro offered brick houses, shops, and streets, indoor baths, and toilets connected to a city-wide sewage system. No one knows why these civilizations disappeared.

About 1500 B.C., Aryans began wandering into India from central Asia, pushing the darker-skinned Dravidians to the south. The Aryans wrote the Vedas, sacred books upon which

Hinduism is founded. Over the centuries, India remained divided into many small kingdoms. But at certain points in history, empires emerged and united large areas of the subcontinent. Both Darius I of Persia and Alexander the Great of Macedonia invaded north India, opening sea and trade routes between Asia and Europe.

Asoka, the greatest Mauryan emperor, united all but the very south of India in 250 B.C. Muslims began to raid India from Afghanistan in A.D. 700, and soon founded small kingdoms on the Gangetic Plain. In 1526, Babir founded the Muslim Mogul Empire. The third Mogul, Akbar the Great, established a peaceful, effective rule over most of India. His grandson, Shah Jahan, built the Taj Mahal in memory of his favorite wife, Mumtaz. Meanwhile, Europeans began establishing trading posts on India's coasts.

The British East India Company became the major European force in India, conquering the country bit by bit. In 1857, Indian soldiers revolted against the British, but after 14 months, their revolt was crushed. The British government took over ruling India, and in 1876, Queen Victoria became Empress of India. India, as part of the British Empire, was called the jewel in the crown of the empress.

Taj Mahal

A tremendous and ornate tomb containing the bodies of 17th-century Indian ruler Shah Jahan and his wife

In their years under British rule, Indians continually struggled to achieve freedom. Finally, in the 1940s, the Indian National Congress won independence for India under the leadership of Mohandas Gandhi and Jawaharlal Nehru, India's first prime minister. At the same time, in 1947, the subcontinent divided into Hindu India and Muslim Pakistan. India and Pakistan continue to struggle with each other for territory.

Indian women carrying water jugs

India also struggles under the burden of a huge population, many of whom live in rural conditions. A visitor to India sees modern industry and technology butting heads with old, traditional ways of life. While some Indian farmers still plow with yokes of oxen, Indian office workers talk with the world through computers and fax machines. India has the largest film industry in the world, a thriving space program, and major chemical, steel, and medical industries. At the same time, ancient temples fill with worshippers offering incense and flowers to traditional gods and goddesses, especially at festival times.

As you might suppose, Indians play many different kinds of games. Clubs offer sparkling lawns for tennis. Schools and colleges compete against each other in everything from American basketball to English cricket to traditional sports like the team tag games of *kabaddi* and *kho-kho*. Children spend recess playing *lagoria* (seven tiles), shooting marbles, and jumping rope. And every year, each state sends its best athletes to the National Games, which feature track and field events. Everywhere you look, India is full of life!

India has a large and successful technology industry; this woman is working in an electronics factory.

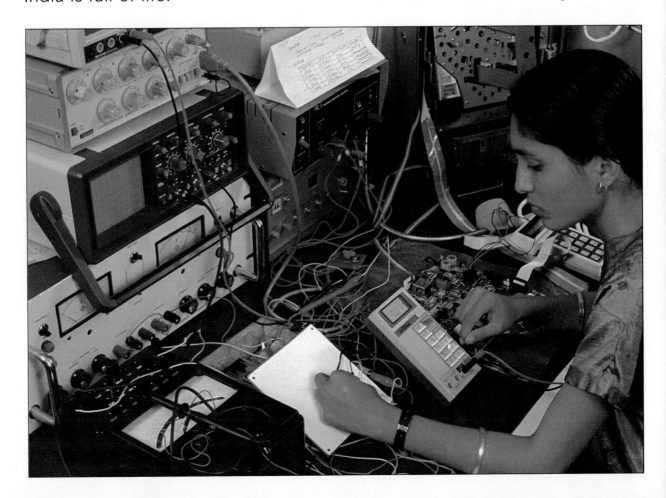

India at a Glance

People

India's population is 900 million people, the second-largest in the world (China is the world's most populous country). India's many people speak 24 major languages and hundreds of dialects. The languages are divided into groups. Aryan languages include Punjabi, Hindi (the national language), Gujarati, and Bengali. Dravidian languages include Malayalam, Tamil, and Telegu.

People of all the world's major religions live in India. About 80 percent of Indians are Hindus, but Muslims, Christians, Sikhs, Buddhists, Jains, Zoroastrians, and Jews also live, work, and worship in India.

Land

The Indian peninsula measures about 2,000 miles (3,219 km) from top to bottom, and almost the same from side to side. Geographers call this peninsula a "subcontinent" because it is so large, and because the Himalayan Mountains separate it from the rest of Asia. Two large countries, India and Pakistan, share this subcontinent, along with the smaller countries of Bangladesh, Bhutan, and Nepal. India occupies about 1.2 million square miles (3.1 million square km), making it one of the largest countries in the world.

Below the Himalayan Mountains, which are the highest in the world, lies the Indo-Gangetic Plain, named for the Indus and Ganges rivers that water it. The Deccan Plateau stretches south, with the Vindhya Mountains and Eastern and Western Ghats forming a triangle around it.

Government

The world's largest democracy, India has regular and openly contested elections. India's written Constitution guarantees equal rights to all citizens, whatever their religion, race, sex, place of birth, or social status. The Constitution says that everyone over 21 years of age can vote. Like Great Britain, on which its government is modeled, India has two houses of Parliament: the *Rajya Subha,* or upper house, and the *Lok Subha,* or "House of the People." The political party with the most elected representatives forms the government and names the prime minister, who runs the government. The prime minister names the chief ministers of government departments.

Each of India's 25 states has its own government, and local town and city governments are also freely elected.

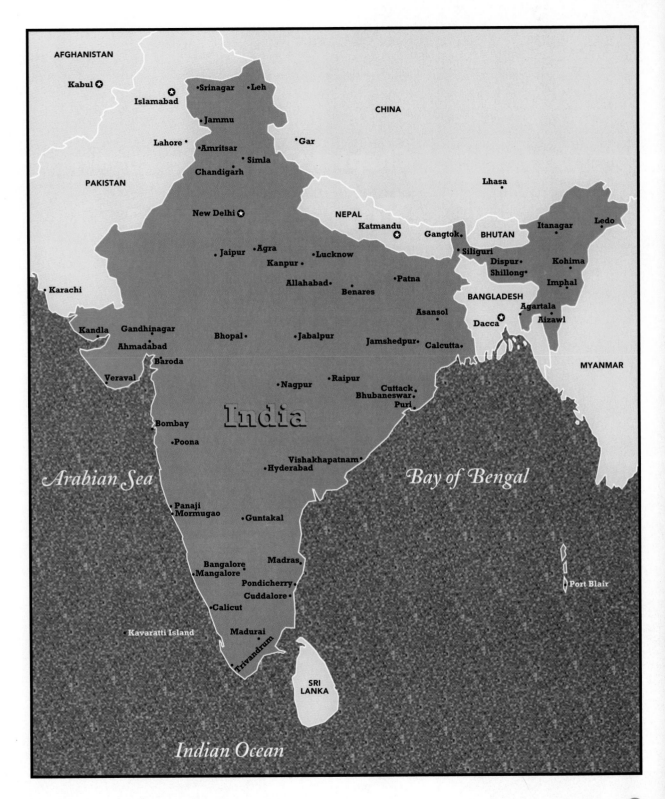

AFGHANISTAN

Kabul ✪

Islamabad ✪

PAKISTAN

Karachi •

Srinagar • • Leh

• Jammu

Lahore • • Amritsar

Chandigarh • Simla

New Delhi ✪

• Jaipur • Agra • Lucknow
Kanpur •

Allahabad • • Benares

CHINA

Lhasa •

NEPAL

Katmandu ✪ Gangtok •

• Gar

Patna •

BHUTAN

Itanagar • Ledo •

• Siliguri
Dispur • Kohima
Shillong • Imphal

BANGLADESH Agartala •
Dacca ✪ Aizawl •

Asansol •

Kandla •

Gandhinagar •

Ahmadabad •

Baroda •

Veraval •

Bhopal • • Jabalpur

Jamshedpur • Calcutta •

MYANMAR

India

• Nagpur • Raipur

Cuttack •
Bhubaneswar •
Puri •

Bombay •

• Poona

Vishakhapatnam •
• Hyderabad

Arabian Sea

Bay of Bengal

• Panaji
• Mormugao

• Guntakal

Bangalore •
• Mangalore

Madras •

Pondicherry •

Port Blair

Cuddalore •

• Calicut

• Kavaratti Island

Madurai •

Trivandrum

SRI
LANKA

Indian Ocean

Chapter One

Yoga Asanas and Surya Namaskar

Over the centuries, Indians developed many kinds of exercises. Most exercises have a specific purpose. Some exercises help people meditate as a part of their religious experience. Others help wrestlers gain strength and flexibility, because wrestling has always been a favorite Indian sport. For example, *dands* (push-ups) develop upper-body strength, while *baithaks* (squats) improve leg strength. But every exercise helps people become and stay healthy.

When people think of India, they often imagine someone sitting cross-legged on the floor, meditating. They are thinking of a *yogi*. A yogi is a person who follows a **yoga**, which means a discipline. The Hindu religion defines many types of yoga for body, mind, and spirit. Body positions associated with yoga are called *asanas*.

A modern yogi

asanas

different body positions
used to do yoga

There are two kinds of asanas — meditative and cultural. When people meditate, they focus their minds and try to relax or gain more control over their bodies. Meditative asanas are exercises that help focus the mind for religious reasons. Some yogis can hold poses for days and weeks, not feeling hunger or thirst. They believe this frees their souls.

People practice cultural asanas for general health, not as part of religious practice. These exercises develop flexibility, posture, and calmness. There are hundreds of these asanas.

Listed below are some easy asanas you can try, but be very careful. Move slowly and carefully, and *never* force any part of your body into a position that doesn't feel comfortable. And don't worry if you can't do a pose on the first try. As with all physical activity, practicing each day makes you better.

Bhujangasana (Cobra Pose)
Lie flat on your stomach with your forehead touching the ground. Bend your elbows so that your hands are on the ground, palms down, beside your head. Raise your head and bend your neck as far up as you can. Arch your back slowly upward, using your hands and arms only to support yourself. Try to feel each vertebra in your spine as you move upward. When you

A man doing a variation of the *Bhujangasana* (cobra) pose

are as far as you can go, you are in the Cobra pose; you look like a cobra ready to strike.

Dhanur Vakrasana (The Bow)

Lie flat on your stomach. Bend your knees to bring your feet toward your head. Reach back around with your hands and grasp your ankles. Gently pull with hands and feet to bend your back into the Bow position.

Halasana (The Plow)

Lie on your back with your arms wrapped around your head. Slowly raise your legs up over your head until they touch the ground behind you. Hold this Plow position for as long as you can. Variations include placing your hands flat on the ground opposite your feet.

More difficult asanas are meant only for experts with countless hours of training and superb flexibility. In the *Soma Asana*, you sit cross-legged with each foot tucked over the opposite leg. The classic *Padmasana* (lotus) positions each foot up over the opposite thigh. From this position, some people can raise themselves up on their hands while keeping their legs crossed. This is *Uttita Padmasana*. Experts can swing their bodies and even walk on their hands while in the Uttita Padmasana position! They also place their hands between their crossed legs, raising their body up off the ground. Even more difficult is the *Urdhva Padmasana*, which is the classic Padmasana, or lotus pose, done upside down, standing on your head!

Some really experienced yogis can place both of their feet behind their heads, supporting themselves with their hands, and "walk" on their hands. Again, this is for expert yogis only. If you tried this on your own, you might get your feet stuck behind your head!

Surya Namaskar began centuries ago as a religious exercise. *Surya* means "sun," and *Namaskar* means "greetings." Even today, many Indians continue to "greet the sun" each morning with this exercise as a part of their religious observances. Others use it simply as a way of keeping healthy.

It takes a lot of strength and training to achieve the *Uttita Padmasana* yoga position.

Surya Namaskar has a long history as an exercise in addition to being a religious practice. In the 17th century, Sivaji, who founded the Maratha Empire, ordered his soldiers to practice it. In the 19th century, Bhavanrao Pant Pratinidhi, the *Raja* (King) of Aundh, made everyone in his country do Surya Namaskar each day. He even determined how many times they were to repeat it. Children between the ages of 8 and 12 had to do 25 to 50 Namaskars daily. Young people between the ages of 12 and 16 were to repeat it 50 to 100 times. Older people were to do even more repetitions. In this way, the raja hoped to have healthy, strong subjects.

"Greeting the sun" in India

Breathing

To do Surya Namaskar correctly, you also have to breathe at the right times! Here's how. Take a deep breath through your nose at position 1. Hold your breath during positions 2, 3, and 4. When your knees, chest, and forehead all touch the ground in position 5, breathe out through your nose. Take another slow breath during position 6, and hold it through 7, 8, and 9. Breathe out again at position 10. You'll have to exercise slowly until you get the hang of it.

Surya Namaskar is not a game, but an exercise of ten counts or positions. If used for religious purposes, it is always done facing the rising sun. For non-Hindus, the exercises provide the benefits of relaxation and stretching tight muscles and limbs. Because eight parts of the body touch the ground during the exercise, Surya Namaskar is also called *Ashtanga Dand* or "Eight Limb Exercise." The eight parts of the body that touch the ground are the forehead, chest, two palms, two knees, and two feet.

Remember: When doing any stretches or exercises, take it easy and don't do anything that hurts.

1   2   3   4   5

1 Stand with your hands flat together in front of your face.

2 Keeping your knees straight, bend your waist and stretch out your hands until your palms touch the ground.

3 Slide your left leg behind your body as far as can while you arch your back.

4 Slide your right leg back until it's beside your left leg. Straighten your back and keep your arms stiff.

5 Now, bend your elbows until your knees, chest, and forehead all touch the ground.

6 Arch your back, pushing your chest forward and looking up as high as you can.

7 Push your knees and hips up in the air as high as you can.

8 Bend your right knee and bring your right foot between your hands. Arch your back as you do this.

9 Bring your left foot beside your right foot, straighten both your knees as you bend your waist.

10 Stand up and stretch your arms high over your head. Finally, return your hands together in front of your face. You're back in position one.

Now repeat the exercise, but this time begin with your right foot in position three. Alternate beginning with your left and right feet each time you do the exercise.

6   7   8   9   10

Chapter Two

Mass Drills, Folk Dances, Combatives

Indians love to celebrate. Each of the Indian peoples developed their own group exercises and folk dances as ways of celebrating together. They celebrate religious festivals, harvests, marriages, and other special occasions.

On national holidays, such as Republic Day, groups from each Indian state gather together to share their mass drills and folk dances. When that happens, music and movement fill the air night and day.

A **baneti** is a baton with at least one ball tied by string to each of its ends. Some baneti are crossed sticks, each with one or more balls tied to its end. Others are wheels with single or crossed bars inside of them as handles and with many balls tied around the outside. Sometimes balls of different colors are tied to baneti to create bands of color as they are twirled around.

Exercisers twirl baneti with their hands and wrists, sometimes in large groups. They spin the baneti in front of their bodies, over their heads, from side to side, and behind their backs. Experts throw and catch spinning baneti in the air and even pass them from person to person. Some people say that the exercises were developed to make lancers quick and skilled with their lances, especially when riding at full gallop. Whatever their origin, baneti may be the forerunners of the batons of American high schools and colleges.

Balancing on the *malcum*, a pillar used for training by wrestlers

The word **lezim** may come from the Persian word for "bow," and a lezim does look something like a bow. It's possible that lezim exercises developed to make archers more skilled. In any case, a lezim is a wooden stick about 18 inches (46 cm) long with a loose iron chain attached to its ends. You hold the lezim by the stick and a handle in the middle of the chain. Thin metal disks attached to the chain make clanging sounds when the chain moves.

Indians use lezim in many different gymnastic and rhythmic exercises, each with its own name and set of commands. By bending and stepping and turning, athletes combine different body and lezim positions while exercising. Indians love to see hundreds of people exercise together in mass drills, with lezims crashing at each count.

To exercise with a lezim, always hold the stick in your left hand and the chain, at its handle, in your right. The basic lezim movement is called *Char Thoke* or "Four Counts." The lezim will make a crashing sound at each count. Start by holding the lezim in front of you, left hand out, right hand near your chest. You look like you're shooting a bow! This position is called *hushar* or "attention." On count 1, bend at your waist and bring your hands together near your toes. On count 2, raise halfway up, bringing the lezim near your waist and quickly pulling the chain

lezim

a stick similar to a bow
used for exercises and
physical training

away from the stick. On count 3, stand up, thrust your right hand (with the chain) in front of you and bring the stick against your right forearm. On count 4, move your left hand (with the stick) in front of you so that you can look through the lezim. Finish by bringing the lezim to your chest, hands together. Rest by holding the lezim with only your right hand at your right side. Carry the lezim over your left shoulder.

Women in Bombay, India, performing a mass exercise drill

Both folk dancers and exercisers use **tipri** sticks. A tipri stick should be about 12 inches (30 cm) long and at least 3/4-inch (1.8 cm) around. Each dancer or athlete holds a tipri in each hand—sometimes two in each hand. They strike their tipri together, and then reach out to strike each others' tipri, as they execute specific steps. Dancers do this to music.

In many typical Indian festivals, people dress in bright and colorful costumes.

The basic tipri "step-and-strike" movement has four counts. (1) From a comfortable standing position, touch your right toe behind your left heel as you strike your right tipri against your left tipri. (2) Step forward with your right foot. (3) Touch your left toe behind your right heel as you strike your tipri together again, right against left. (4) Step forward with your left foot. All dance and exercise steps follow from this simple rhythm. For example, next time strike your tipri above your head on (1) and near the ground on (3). Then form two circles of dancers, one within a larger one. Going in opposite directions, reach out to hit each others' tipri on count (3). Many, many variations and colorful folk dances result.

Most ancient Asian people developed different types of martial arts, ways in which to defend themselves or attack others. The Japanese have many martial arts, such as *judo* and *karate*, while the Koreans have *tai-kwan-do*. Indians developed their own martial arts.

A thin bamboo stick about 5 feet (1.5 m) long and 1 inch (2.5 cm) thick, a **lathi** can be a weapon. Indeed, Indian police receive lathi training and scatter mobs with the famous "lathi charge." Experts can twirl a lathi fast enough to deflect a thrown knife. Even so, many Indians just exercise with lathi.

Carry a lathi by hooking your left hand around the thinner end and passing the stick behind your left armpit. This is the *lapet* position. At the command *arum* (at ease), bring the lathi horizontal, grip it with both hands near each other, and then place one end on the ground. At *hushar* (attention), swing the lathi around, upright. And at *pavitra hushar,* take a step forward, bend your knees, and point the lathi forward a bit.

From pavitra hushar, you can swing the lathi in circles, right or left, while standing, stepping forward or backward, or turning around. Many such swings and steps make up a lathi drill. And each position can become part of a lathi fight, should that become necessary.

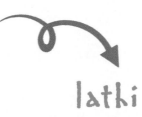

lathi

a bamboo stick that can be used as a weapon and is manipulated in many positions for lathi drills

Indian women in the 1950s
practicing with spears

Indians developed **fari-gadka** as a safe way to practice for sword fights. The fari is a leather shield about 9 inches (22 cm) around. A gadka is a leather-covered wooden stick, about 36 inches (90 cm) long, with a covered handle. Exercises with fari-gadka need two combatives striking at each other, catching the blows with either fari or gadka—or both. Footwork is critical to successful drills, as combatives move up and down, left and right, and twirl around. Of course, Indians have named each cut and thrust with the gadka and each catch and parry with the fari. They practice each movement many times.

As is true of most Indian combative exercises, fari-gadka developed into folk dances. Sometimes dancers, as well as combatants demonstrating their skill, use real swords and shields. Sparks fly as metal clangs against metal! It is also true that the British, when they ruled India, banned societies that taught and practiced swordplay, because members became so skilled in this deadly art.

Indians love the sport of wrestling. Over the centuries they have developed many exercises to give wrestlers strength and agility. Wrestlers lift stone and wooden weights, called *nal* and *sumtola*, to gain strength. They swing heavy Indian clubs for strong and supple arms. Most unusual are exercises done on the **malcum**, or "wrestlers' pillar." Found only in India, malcum became a sport in itself.

Two men wrestling in a town's public square

Made of *sheeshum* or teak wood, a large malcum stands 7 feet (2.1 m) from the ground. It tapers from about 21 inches (53 cm) up to 27 inches (69 cm) around. Near the top, there is a long handle and knob. A thin malcum stands 11 feet (3.4 m) high. Large or thin, about 4 feet (1.2 m) of the malcum lies underground.

A daredevil balances atop a malcum.

To mount the pillar, athletes grip the malcum with both hands behind their heads, swing their feet up over their heads, and grip the malcum between their legs. Letting go their hands, they twist around, up and down the pillar, gripping it with hands, legs, thighs, and feet in different holds. Experts balance on top, either on their feet, hands, back, or stomach. Sometimes several athletes climb a pillar together to present group poses.

Daredevils climb malcum set on tables. Sometimes the legs of the table balance on bottles, and sometimes those bottles stand on another table balanced on bottles. Experts tie swords to a malcum or plant them, blade up, in the ground around it. Holding knives in their hands and teeth, they run toward the pillar, jump, turn in midair, and catch the malcum between their thighs!

Boys and young men climb
the malcum in Bombay.

Indians also exercise and perform stunts on
smaller malcum hung on rope from a frame.
Some work on a small "inclined" malcum
balanced on the ground. Others exercise and
pose on hanging strips of cane.

Chapter Three

Team-Tag Games

C hildren all over the world play tag. Someone is "it" and tries to touch, or tag, other players. Sometimes a tagged player becomes "it," and sometimes a tagged player is out of the game. Indians play team tag games, and each one has a special twist. Two of these games are *kabaddi* and *kho-kho*.

All across India, in dusty village fields, on sandy riverbanks, and on city playgrounds, hardy souls play the rough sport of **kabaddi**. Kabaddi is played on a court 40 feet (12 m) long and 25-32 feet (7.6-9.7 m) wide. A midline divides the court into two 20-foot (6-m) sections. Eight feet (2.4 m) on either side of the midline is a "baulk line." One team at a time sends a "raider" across the midline to try and tag members of the other team, who are called "anti-raiders" or "antis," for short. A raider must cross the antis' baulk line and return across the midline to complete a turn—and the raider must do this in one breath! But how do you know the raider completes a turn in one breath? You know because the raider must make a continuous sound, repeating a word or syllable the whole time. So, crossing the midline, the raider begins the "cant," saying, "Kabaddi, kabaddi, kabaddi..."

"kabaddi
kabaddi
kabaddi
kabaddi"

or a similar word. (In fact, other names for kabaddi result from other cants used, like "hu-tu-tu," "chadu kudu," "ha-du-du," and "do-do-do.")

Then the fun begins, as the raider tries to tag antis, and they try to "tackle" him until he runs out of breath before recrossing the midline! The game looks like a fight between a mongoose and a cobra. The raider dances back and forth, left and right, like a mongoose seeking a soft spot to bite, throwing out a foot now, and then a hand. The antis, spread out across the court, move backward and forward in a line as the raider approaches and backs off. They look like the cobra, waiting to strike. Unlike a cobra, though, when they strike, they hold on, while the raider tries to tag and run.

Antis catch a raider in a *kabaddi* match.

If an anti touches a raider and the raider loses the cant before recrossing the midline, the raider is out. But, if the raider touches any (or all!) antis and successfully returns across the midline, all touched antis are out. It doesn't matter who touches whom, and a raider who touches an anti need not cross the antis' baulk line.

Teams score 10 points for every opponent put out, an extra 20 if the entire side of nine players is out within a time period. When the last player on a team is out, the entire team returns, and play continues. A game consists of two 20-minute halves, and the team with the most points at the end of play wins the game.

A large crowd gathers to watch *kabaddi*.

Introduced as a "demonstration sport" at the 1936 Olympics in Berlin, kabaddi is becoming an international sport. Since 1970, the Amateur Kabaddi Federation of India has held national championships. The Asian Kabaddi Federation formed in 1978 to organize the first Asian championship. Nepal and Bangladesh sent teams to compete with India. Now the World Kabaddi Championship Organization, based in Canada, plans World Kabaddi Cup tournaments. Watch out — kabaddi is coming!

Indian girls playing
kho-kho during a recent
National Games

In **kho-kho**, players on the chasing, or "it," team cannot cross a center line, while the "runners" on the other team can! Also, chasers cannot change the direction they first take, but runners can.

Kho-kho is played on a court that measures 111 by 51 feet (33.8 by 15.5 m). Two posts mark each end of the center line. Twelve-inch (30-cm) wide crosslines cut the center line at 8-foot (2.4-m) intervals. A "chaser" squats on each crossline, facing the opposite way from teammates on either side. The ninth chaser waits by a pole for the game to begin. Three runners from the other team gather by the other pole. When the referee blows a whistle, the chaser runs the length of the court, and the game is on.

The chaser tries to tag the runners, but when a runner crosses the center line, the chaser cannot follow. Instead, the chaser "gives kho" to a teammate facing that direction. The chaser does this by touching the teammate with a hand and saying "kho" so that all can hear. The teammate then takes off after the runners, while the first chaser squats down in the now empty space. Another rule says that the teammate must continue in the direction, left or right, first taken from the crossline he or she was sitting on. The runner, of course, can switch directions or "double back" across the center line—but the chaser must give kho to teammates in order to switch directions or cross the line. Both runners and chasers can go around the endposts. It all happens fast and it's great fun!

"kho!"

"kho!"

"kho!"

When touched by a chaser, a runner is out and must leave the court. When all three runners are out, three more take their places. As in kabaddi, chasers score 10 points for each runner put out and 20 points for putting out the entire nine-person team within a time period. Kho-kho consists of five- to seven-minute innings, and two innings make a game. Of course, teams switch being chasers and runners between innings.

Chapter Four

Children's Games

hildren all over the world play **marbles**. Indians play many variations, depending on local customs. One of these games uses a hole dug in front of a wall or tree. Children who can't afford marbles collect pin-pinya seeds, which are hard, white seeds from the pin-pinya tree of North India. By dipping seeds in black or blue or red ink, players are able to tell their seeds apart.

In the one-hole game, players contribute several marbles or pin-pinyas into a bunch, and then take turns throwing the bunch toward the hole. A player keeps any that fall into the hole, and then tries to capture more by throwing another marble or seed at the bunch. But he must hit only those that opponents point out. Failure to land any marble or seed in the hole or hit the "target" marble means a lost turn.

A marble player shoots at an opponent's marble.

shooter

the one marble a player uses
to hit other marbles

To play another marble game, players dig three holes in a row, 3 to 5 feet (0.9 to 1.5 m) from each other, and draw a line about 10 feet (3 m) from the first hole. Players take turns throwing their "shooter" marble from the line to the first hole. A player whose marble lands in the first hole continues play by aiming at the second hole. Players must now shoot their marble off a finger, keeping their thumb on the ground. Each player's turn continues as long as they shoot into a hole. They can also shoot at an opponent's marble, trying to knock it as far away from the playing area as possible, and then continue their turn. Players go from hole to hole and back again until they make ten holes and their shooter becomes "poisonous." If a poisonous marble strikes any opponent's marble, the opponent is "dead" and out of the game.

It's not enough for Indians to buy and spin **tops**; they've invented a number of games to play with them. An Indian top, made of teak or blackwood, has a round head, lines cut around its tapered end, and a metal spike for a point. It comes with a strong string. To spin it, you hold one end of the string at the head, wind it around the spike, and then continue winding the string around and around the lines, working your way up to the head. Loop the free end of the string around a finger, hold the top

Spinning a top on a Bombay, India, playground

between your thumb and fingers, and snap it toward the ground to spin it. It takes practice, and everyone has a special method of spinning a top. Spinning a top directly into your hand is called *hat-jali*, and it begins most games. (Less able players must spin their tops on the ground, and then loop their strings around the spinning tops to flip them up into their hands.)

In one game, the last person to hat-jali must put a top into the center of a circle. Other players try to knock that top out of the circle by spinning their tops into it. If they fail to spin their tops, touch the target top, or spin out of the circle, they must add their tops to the circle. Play continues until all tops are caught in the circle or knocked out of it, at which point everyone must hat-jali again to determine whose top begins inside the circle. Of course, everyone has their own variations of this game, and experts try not only to knock a top out of the circle, but to split it by spinning their tops directly on top of it!

In side streets and on playgrounds all over India, you will find children throwing a ball at a pile of tiles. When the ball hits the pile, tiles and children scatter everywhere. They're playing **lagoria**. To play lagoria, children make seven tiles of decreasing size from about 5 inches (13 cm) to about 2 inches (5 cm) across. Although some make lagoria from wood, most use broken flowerpots or flat stones. They stack the tiles in a pyramid shape, the largest on the bottom. They also use a ball about the size of a tennis ball.

Players draw a line 15 to 20 feet (4.5 to 6 m) from the lagoria, and then chose up sides. One

lagoria

a game in which players
attempt to knock over tiles
by throwing a ball at them

side will be fielders while the other throws. Throwing-team members take turns throwing the ball at the pile of tiles, trying to knock it over. Each thrower has three chances, unless a fielder catches the ball after one bounce. If that happens, another member of the throwing team takes over. If all throwers are caught out without hitting the lagoria, the teams switch positions.

When a thrower hits the lagoria, scattering the tiles, his or her team tries to rebuild the pile without being hit by the ball. The fielding team, of course, finds the ball and throws it at them. Fielders can pass the ball but not run with it. They can also try to hit the tiles, spoiling efforts to rebuild them. If they hit a throwing-team member, the teams switch positions for a new round of the game. If the throwing team succeeds in rebuilding the pile of tiles without anyone being hit, team members call out "Lagoria" or "Seven Tiles" and score a point. They continue as the throwing team. At the end of play, which is usually when it gets dark or someone's mother calls them home to eat, the team with the most points wins.

guli danda

a game in which players take turns hitting a small stick pointed at both ends

Long before the English invented cricket or Americans thought up baseball, Indians played **guli danda**, and variations of the game are everywhere. Usually played by two persons, teams of four to six play some variations.

The game requires a *guli* (called an *iti* in South India), which is a small stick at least 1 inch (2.8 cm) around and 4 to 6 inches (10 to 15 cm) long, sharpened at both ends. Players also need a *danda*, a stick up to 2 inches (5 cm) around and about 18 inches (45 cm) long. Near one end of a large, flat field, players dig a small trench in the ground, just deep and long enough for the guli to rest in.

Play begins when each player, in turn, places the guli across the trench. Scraping the danda through the trench behind the guli, they flip it as far as possible. (This action is called *kolane*.) Some players sharpen one end of their danda for this flip. Others use thin, wiry sticks as special flipping sticks. The player who flips the guli farthest goes first and again flips the guli from the trench into the playing area. This time other players try to catch it, putting the first player out. If the guli lands on the ground, the first player puts the danda across the trench, and an opposing player throws the guli at it. Hitting the danda or landing the guli in the trench also puts the first player out. If neither happens, the first player continues play by hitting a pointed end of the guli with the danda so that the guli flips into the air, and then hitting the guli as hard as possible. After three of these hits, the player again places the danda across the trench, then estimates how many lengths of the danda lie between trench and guli. Each danda length counts as a point. The player scores these points unless the opponent, throwing the guli in, hits the danda or lands in the trench.

Opposing players can challenge the number of points the first player claims. If they do, the first player must measure off the distance between trench and guli with the danda. If the guli is equal to or farther away than the distance claimed, the player wins those points and begins the next series of three hits from that position. (In some variations, the player gets to double or triple those points.) If the guli is closer than the estimated distance, the first player is out and loses those points from his or her total score. It's the next player's turn. The player with the most points after an equal number of turns wins.

Team games are played on a field marked with lines to indicate the distance the guli travels and define the area in which it must safely land.

An Indian kite market

What's the best way to celebrate a cool winter evening? Fly and fight **kites**! A favorite pastime of Indian royalty, kite fighting still provokes strong passions in fierce intercity championships.

Made of delicate paper stretched over thin strips of bamboo, Indian kites (*pattangs*) come in different sizes and colors. Their diamond shape means they move quickly through the air, responding instantly to a kite-flier's control.

Fighters apply a mixture of glass powder (*lugale*) and boiled rice or egg yolk to string (*sadhi*) to make sharp string, called *manja*. They wind the string around churkees, putting the manja at the top so it's nearest the kite. When fighting, fliers maneuver their kites so that their manja crosses another flier's sadhi in midair. Quickly pulling the kite downward (which is called *khench*) or letting it out into the wind (called sailly), fighters make their string rub quickly across the other's with enough friction to cut it, setting the other kite free. A cut kite can be claimed by anyone who catches it.

Really great fighters work in teams. One teammate fights while the other flies downwind. The second flier's kite replaces the manja with pieces of wire hooked together. When a fighting kite is cut, this teammate can catch it in midair by circling it until the wire catches the cut kite's string. The flier then pulls both kites out of the air!

Cricket came to India with the British—and stayed. In fact, the Calcutta Cricket Club, founded by the British in 1792, is the oldest cricket club outside of the United Kingdom. Most schools and colleges field cricket teams, and India has become an international cricket power.

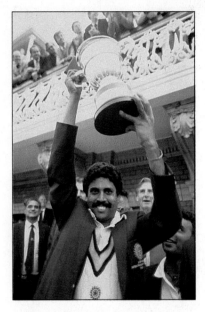

Above: Kapil Dev, a legend of Indian cricket

International matches, called "Tests," last up to five days. Nine countries—England, India, Pakistan, Australia, New Zealand, South Africa, Sri Lanka, Zimbabwe, and the West Indies—now have full Test status. Kenya, the United Arab Emirates, and the Netherlands hold associate status. These countries play each other in single Tests, and they all play in World Cup cricket tournaments. India, Pakistan, and Sri Lanka cohost the 1996 World Cup.

India's Test captains, or "skippers," have been world-famous cricketers. The 1960s hailed Mensur Ali Khan, the Nawab of Pataudi, as a top bowler. Recently retired skipper Sunil Gavaskar holds the record for most runs scored in Test matches. Another player, bowler Kapil Dev, became the highest "wicket-taker" in Test history in 1994.

India plays England in a 1993
Test match.

But how do you play cricket? It's rather involved, but let's just say that teams take turns batting and fielding the ball. One fielder, the bowler, throws the ball (without bending the elbow) at a wicket, which is three sticks set up 22 yards (20 m) away. There are fast bowlers, spin bowlers, and pace bowlers, depending on how they bowl. A batsman defends the wickets and tries to score runs by hitting the ball into the field and running the 22 yards. Score one point for every run. A batsman is out if a bowled ball knocks down a wicket or a hit ball is caught. Teams take turns batting, and they don't have to let every person on their team bat. It depends on the score and the condition of the field, or pitch. Teams win by having more points when their opponents have batted around twice, within the allotted time. And, of course, everyone stops for tea.

Playing cricket on a city street in India

Asians may have invented **field hockey**, but Europeans have also played it for centuries. In 1886, England formed its Hockey Association and established rules. In 1928, the Indian Hockey Association began.

A goalie for the Indian national field hockey team

To play hockey, you need two teams of 11 players each. Players use a curved hockey stick to dribble and pass a hard ball to each other. They score goals by hitting the ball into their opponent's goal. Only the flat part of the hockey stick can touch the ball, but players can stop it with their hands. Goalies may kick the ball inside the goal area (called the "D").

India dominated international hockey in the first half of this century. It won the gold medal in every Olympics held between 1928 and 1956. In 1960, India lost to Pakistan in the finals and had to settle for the second-place silver. Since then, Pakistan, the Netherlands, Germany, and South Korea have become hockey powers. In fact, Pakistan won the eighth World Cup hockey tournament held in Australia in

December 1994, beating the Netherlands in the finals. India finished fifth. Nonetheless, the best player of all times was India's Dyan Chand, who took gold medals in the 1928, 1932, and 1936 Olympics. Called "the wizard of hockey," Dyan became the hockey coach of India's National Institute of Sports. Other great players include Kanwar "Babu" Singh, who won Olympic gold in 1948 and 1952, and Balbir Singh, whose gold medals came in 1952 and 1956.

India (in blue jerseys) plays the USSR in field hockey at the 1988 Summer Olympics.

According to Indian sportswriters, **badminton** originated in the city of Pune years ago. The British took the game to England, founding "Poona" clubs in which to play it. (Poona is the old, British way of spelling Pune.) People in the town of Badminton, in Gloucestershire, loved the game so much that other Britishers started calling the game after their town. So it is "badminton" to this day. People all over India play badminton. Many play on lighted outside courts in cool, winter evenings. Major tournaments are held on these and indoor courts.

Badminton is a very popular game in India.

Although **tennis** may have started in France, an Englishman, Major Wingfield, set rules in 1874 that established the modern game. The British soon brought tennis to India, where it became a fixture of colonial life. Every major city had an officers' club, and every officers' club had a tennis court. The best clubs sported fine grass courts that Indian *malis* maintained, clipping and rolling them by hand. Hill stations, where the British moved in summertime to get out of the hot plains, had rolled dirt and clay courts.

Every Thursday afternoon, the British had tea together as they watched each other play tennis. It was the social event for that day. Indians soon learned the game, and tennis continues to be a major club sport in India as elsewhere in the world. Several Indian tennis players have reached international levels of play, and India does well in Davis Cup play, which is a contest between teams from different countries.

Ramanathan Krishnanan (top)
and son Ramesh (bottom)

Ramanathan Krishnanan and his son, **Ramesh**, both achieved international recognition in tennis. Ramanathan was a star of the fifties. His best performance came in the 1960 Wimbledon tournament, the premier Grand Slam tennis event held every year at the All England Lawn Tennis and Croquet Club. That year Ramanathan reached the semifinals. Other players enjoyed watching Ramanathan play because of his smooth tennis stroke. His son, Ramesh, also played on the international tour, although without his father's success. Recently, Vijay Amritraj and Leander Paes have risen in international play.

Volleyball came to India with the worldwide spread of the Y.M.C.A. (Young Men's Christian Association). As Y's were founded in major Indian cities, members learned the new game. During World War II, Americans stationed in India also played the game. Indians loved it, and soon students at schools and colleges all over the country were playing volleyball after school for fun and—in tournaments against students from other schools—for prestige.

Basketball also came to India through the Y.M.C.A. and American servicemen. Early Indian courts, made of packed dirt or concrete, were outside, with hoops set in wooden backboards. Now, more and more institutions have indoor courts.

People call **polo** "the sport of kings"—probably because you need to be as rich as a king to afford a stable of polo ponies! In any case,

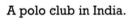
A polo club in India.

Indian rajas and their cavalry officers developed polo. The Moghal emperor Akbar loved the sport.

Elephant polo is a popular amusement in India.

Riding on horseback, polo players carry a long, flexible stick with a leather strap on the handle and a malletlike head. The strap goes around a wrist so they don't lose the stick as they bend from their pony at a gallop to strike a wooden ball, trying to hit it toward a teammate or through the opponents' goal. A hard, fast game, polo consists of eight 7$\frac{1}{2}$-minute periods, called "chukkers" (rounds). Polo ponies must be fast, quick, and durable—and they are highly prized. But some Indian rajas preferred a slower game and played polo from the backs of elephants!

Indians also play "the world's game"—**soccer football**—but without the national passion of some countries in Europe and South America. Still, most schools and colleges field soccer teams and contest matches vigorously. The Bengal professional league developed strong club players in the 1940s and 1950s, when soccer became hot in Calcutta, but India has not fared well in international play.

India has been well-represented in **track and field** at Asian and Commonwealth games. It dominated the 1951 Asian Games, winning the men's 100, 200, 800, and 1500-meter races, the 1600-meter relay, 5k and 10k walks, the marathon, shot put, and discus! Indian women won the 400-meter relay in 1954.

Milka Singh

Milka Singh (left) became the greatest Indian track star of all time. Called "the Flying Sikh," he may also have been the most graceful sprinter ever. Watching Milka run gave spectators a special thrill. He was truly "poetry in motion."

A village boy from the Punjab, Milka joined the Indian Army at 16. He began running in army races and soon reached national prominence, setting records at 200 and 400 meters. At the international level, he won the U.S.A. Helms Award as the best Asian athlete.

In 1958, Milka took the gold medal at the Commonwealth Games in Cardiff, Wales, with a record time of 46.6 seconds for 440 yards (400 meters). Between 1957 and 1960, he ran more 400s under 47 seconds than anyone else, setting the pace for world-class sprinters. Expected to bring India its first Olympic track-and-field medal, Milka finished a close fourth at the Rome games in 1960. Sportswriters called the final race the fastest 400 meters ever, because the top finishers shattered the previous world record.

As part of its efforts to improve India's showing in international competition, the government wanted to improve the expertise of Indian coaches. To do so, it founded a **National Institute of Sports** staffed by the best coaches from countries around the world. These coaches share their knowledge and techniques with Indian athletes and coaches.

The Institute began operations in March, 1961, in Yadavindra Stadium in the city of Patiala in the Punjab. It also used surrounding sports fields and the city cricket pitch for classes. The international coaches stayed in the small Baradari Palace, once a guest house of the Maharaja of Patiala. But larger and better space would be needed for a full-scale program. Fortunately, Motibagh Palace, the former palace of the Maharaja of Patiala, became available, and everyone moved into it.

Motibagh had pink domes and red-latticed windows, 300 marble rooms and halls, offices and banquet halls, a library and a swimming pool, apartments, trophy and game rooms, a movie theater—you name it! The maharaja's private office became the wrestling gymnasium; his wardrobe room, the gymnastics hall.

His father's harem (where the former maharaja's 150 "wives" had lived) housed students, while coaches lived in the guest apartments. The 300-acre (121-hectare) lawn, with its 9-hole golf course, became hockey and soccer and cricket fields. A courtyard became a volleyball court—and plenty of space remained.

To this amazing "palace of sport" came world-famous coaches. M. P. Pimenov, Grand Master of Sport and former captain of Russia's world champions, came to teach volleyball. Another Grand Master and Olympic champion, Senebledze, coached gymnastics. England's former soccer goalie, Henry Wright; Australian cricketer L. P. O'Brien; Iranian wrestler Amir Hamidi; and Malasian badminton star Cheng Kon Leong also arrived at Motibagh Palace. Of course, India looked to its own Swami Jaganath, and then Dyan Chand, to coach field hockey. Art Howard, an American missionary, coached track and field, assisted by Josh Culbreath, former holder of the 400-meter world record. A retired Indian Army officer, Lt. Gen. Sant Singh, directed the entire operation.

From these beginnings, the National Institute of Sports has thrived, sending graduates all over India and to many countries worldwide.

lossary

asanas
body positions developed either for meditation by religious people or for health by athletes; each position is an asan

baithaks
exercises designed to strengthen the legs; deep-knee bends

baneti
batons or wheels with balls tied to them by string

Bhujangasana (Cobra Pose)
an asan that resembles a cobra ready to strike

cant
a repeated phrase or chant

curry
a mixture of spices used to flavor food

danda
the thick stick used as a bat in guli danda

dands
exercises designed to strengthen biceps and chest; push-ups

Dhanur Vakrasana (The Bow)
an asan that resembles a bow

guli
a small stick, pointed at each end, hit for distance in guli danda

hat-jali
spinning a top directly onto your hand

Halasana (The Plow)
an asan that resembles a wooden plow

harem
quarters for a raja's or maharaja's many wives

Hinduism
the religion of Hindus that began in India

lagoria
Hindi name for the game "Seven Tiles"

lathi
a thin bamboo stick about 5 feet (1.5 m) long, used in martial exercises and as a weapon

mali
an Indian gardener and groundskeeper

Muslim
having to do with Islam, the religion founded by the prophet Mohammed in Arabia

nal
a stone dumbbell used for weight-lifting exercises

Padmasana (lotus)
the classic yoga position of sitting cross-legged with your feet high on the opposite thigh

raja
Hindi word meaning "king"; a *maharaja* is a "great king"; a *rani* is a raja's wife

rickshaw
a passenger carriage powered by foot, bicycle chain, or motorcycle

sadhu
a wandering holy man who goes from temple to temple

sari
woman's dress made of 6 yards (5.5 m) of cloth wound around the waist with one end thrown over a shoulder

Soma Asana
an asan of sitting cross-legged

sumtola
a weight carved out of wood

Surya Namaskar ("Greeting to the Sun")
a ten-position exercise done while breathing and holding your breath at specific times; religious Hindus use it to greet the rising sun

tipri
a stick about 12 inches (30 cm) long and 3/4-inch (1.8 cm) thick, used in rhythmic dances and exercises

tonga
a horse-drawn carriage

Urdhva Padmasana
the lotus asan upside down

Uttita Padmasana
the lotus asan held while "standing" or "walking" on your hands

yoga
Hindi word meaning "discipline," also refers to the various body positions developed for health or meditation

yogi
a Hindu religious person who practices yoga for meditation and spiritual reasons

For Further Reading

Cumming, David. **The Ganges Delta and its People.** New York: Thomson Learning, 1994.

Dhanjal, Beryl. **Amritsar.** New York: Dillon Press, 1994.

Eastaway, Robert. **Cricket Explained.** New York: St. Martins Press 1992.

Ganeri, Anita. **The Indian Subcontinent.** New York: Franklin Watts, 1994.

Ganeri, Anita and Rachel Wright. **India.** New York: Franklin Watts, 1994.

Hermes, Jules. **The Children of India.** Minneapolis: Carolrhoda, 1993.

India in Pictures. Prepared by the Geography Department, Lerner Publications Company. Minneapolis: Lerner Publications Company, 1992.

Lewin, Ted. **Sacred River.** New York: Clarion Books, 1994.

McNair, Sylvia. **India.** Chicago: Children's Press, 1990.

Sherrow, Victoria. **Mohadmas Ghandi: The Power of the Spirit.** Brookfield: Millbrook Press, 1994.

Singha, Rina and Reginald Massey. **India Dances.** New York: George Braziller, Inc., 1967.

Tengrove, Alan. **The Story of the Davis Cup.** London: Stanley Paul & Company, Ltd., 1985.

Wallechinsky, David. **The Complete Book of the Olympics, 1992 edition.** New York: Little Brown, 1991.

Watson, Janne Werner. **India Celebrates.** Champaign, Illinois: Garrard Publishing, 1992.

Williams, Lee Ann. **Basic Field Hockey Strategy.** New York: Doubleday, 1978.

Index

(**Boldface** page numbers indicate illustrations.)

Author's Dedication

To my father, Arthur W. Howard, remembering all those frosty Indian mornings when I watched you coach.

About the Author

Dale Howard was born and raised in India, where his parents served as missionaries. He spent much of his childhood accompanying his father, a coach and teacher of physical education, to Indian sporting events; as an adult, Dale still loves the games he watched and played in India.

Dale Howard worked for 20 years at Open Court Publishing in language arts and curriculum development. He then received his Master of Divinity degree from Luther Seminary in St. Paul, Minnesota. He now serves a church in Minneapolis as associate pastor.

Rev. Howard is married and has four children who are active in various types of sports.

Photo Credits

Cover, ©Satish Parashar/Dinodia Picture Agency; 1, ©Satish Parashar/ Dinodia Picture Agency (top left), ©David Cannon/Allsport (top right), ©Dinodia Picture Agency (bottom); 2–3, ©P. R. Gansham/Dinodia Picture Agency; 4, ©Ravi Shekhar/Dinodia Picture Agency; 5, ©Ashvin Mehta/ Dinodia Picture Agency; 6, ©R. A. Acharya/Dinodia Picture Agency; 8, ©UPI/Bettmann Newsphotos; 9, ©Dinodia Picture Agency; 12, ©Dinodia Picture Agency; 13, ©Anil A. Dave/Dinodia Picture Agency; 15, ©Dinodia Picture Agency; 16, ©Dinodia Picture Agency; 17, ©Anil A. Dave/Dinodia Picture Agency; 20, ©Anil A. Dave/Dinodia Picture Agency; 21, ©Milind Ketkar/Dinodia Picture Agency; 23, ©Suresh G. Gayan/Dinodia Picture Agency; 24, ©N. M. Jain/Dinodia Picture Agency; 26, ©UPI/Bettmann; 27, ©Dinodia Picture Agency; 28, ©Dinodia Picture Agency; 29, ©Suresh G. Gavali/Dinodia Picture Agency; 30, ©Gray Mortimore/Allsport; 32, ©Gray Mortimore/Allsport; 33, ©Milind Ketkar/Dinodia Picture Agency; 34, ©Milind Ketkar/Dinodia Picture Agency; 36, ©Pramod Mistry/Dinodia Picture Agency; 37, ©Satish Parashar/Dinodia Picture Agency; 39, ©Nihalchand Jain/Dinodia Picture Agency; 44, ©Pramod Mistry/Dinodia Picture Agency; 45, ©Pramod Mistry/Dinodia Picture Agency; 46, ©Ben Radford/Allsport; 47, ©Adrian Murrell/Allsport; 48, ©Viren Desai/Dinodia Picture Agency; 49, ©Adrian Murrell/Allsport; 50, ©David Cannon/Allsport; 51, ©Gray Mortimore/Allsport; 52, ©R. A. Ashary/Dinodia Picture Agency; 53 (top), ©AP/Wide World Photos; 53 (bottom), ©Trevor Jones/Allsport; 54, ©Sanjay M. Marathe/Dinodia Picture Agency; 55, ©Dinodia Picture Agency; 56 (top), ©Jason Lauré; 56 (bottom), ©Milind A. Ketkar/Dinodia Picture Agency; 57, ©AP/Wide World Photos